BRITISH LARGE FOWL

By
Michael Roberts

D1390015

Photographs By
John Tarren

© 1994 Michael Roberts
Published by The Domestic Fowl Research
Printed by Bartlett & Son, Swan Yard, St Thomas, Exeter, Devon.
Tel. (01392) 254086

Contents

PREFACE

One of the great difficulties of putting this book together has been to decide which breeds should be included as "British". Since all domestic chickens have been imported into this country over the centuries and have been created by man somewhere, in all honesty there are no breeds which can be called indigenous. Having said that, there are breeds which have been created and improved in this country, mainly from the 1800's onwards and whose originators were British. To take an example of creating another colour of an established breed, which is not quite the same thing as creating a new breed, the Leghorn, a Mediterranean breed from Italy, was taken to America, improved to produce a first class egg layer, imported back to Europe and thence to England, where the Exchequer Leghorn (colour evenly black and white like a chequer board) was made by a breeder in Dumfries in the 1930's. It is a little bit like saying that a Charolais beef cow is British because it has been so long in this country, when clearly its origins are French. What is also confusing is that some of the obviously foreign breeds have a British Standard which is different from the standard of their original country, e.g. Marans from France. So, the breeds which have been included are not only those created in Britain but those developed here over several decades. The British Standards may be found in the book "British Poultry Standards", published by Blackwells.

Michael Roberts
1994

INTRODUCTION

Since the early history of Great Britain, birds have played their part as a provider for man. The Celts would have taken goslings from the indigenous greylag geese. These would have readily imprinted onto humans as it is the flock instinct to associate strongly with whoever appears to be a parent. The goslings would have flourished as they were consuming food (grass) which was not in conflict with man and they would have provided eggs and meat, fat or tallow for lamps and various medicinal uses, flight feathers for arrows and decoration and down feathers for clothing and bedding. The bones would have been used for sewing needles, handles and ornaments, witchcraft and crude musical instruments.

It was not until the early invasions, missionaries and traders that chickens were first introduced into the British Isles. Hens, not being primarily grazers, needed more settled people or farmers because of their food requirements. There is no documentation on early British fowl until the Romans arrived and found poultry were used more for entertainment than as a source of food.

The Romans obviously introduced hens not only for meat and eggs but as watchdogs and time pieces, cock crow being one of the watches of the night. As travel and trade increased, so more selected birds began to appear and regional variations were created. Their ability to thrive in certain areas together with egg production and/or fighting spirit gradually formed a certain pattern of colouring, type and size. Human selection, geography and genetic deprivation also played their part.

These regional breeds were greatly enhanced by the influx of new breeds introduced by traders from the New World during the 1500's. Improved methods of husbandry together with better farming techniques produced adequate table birds, egg producers and sporting birds.

As the human population gradually increased, so the flocks increased in size on the outskirts of towns to cope with the demand of the urban dwellers. By the 1700's many distinct breeds had appeared and a number were documented.

By the middle of the 1800's three important events changed poultry completely. First, the coming of the railways. Second, the banning of cockfighting. Third, the introduction of the Asiatic breeds.

The railways opened up the countryside, providing fast and

easy access to urban markets, and more competition between the various regions for eggs and meat; in this way the serious race began which continues today (worldwide) to find the breed of chicken that lays most eggs or the breed that grows fastest and heaviest.

The banning of cockfighting in 1849 was a serious blow to gentry, traders and publicans, in fact everyone was involved, from magistrates down to schoolboys. The innovation of exhibiting fowl took over from this bloody sport and much of its energy, and great interest was taken in improving and showing some of the regional fowl, as well as the newly imported ones, particularly the Asiatic breeds, the like and size of which had not been seen before.

The arrival of the Asiatic breeds such as the Brahmas, Cochins, Malays and Silkies started a craze of crossing breeds for commercial gain and for extraordinary looks.   Bantams were imported from the Far East and became popular not only because of their appearance but also because they were used to miniaturise existing large breeds and create yet another exhibiting aspect.

Today, the great poultry shows such as The National Poultry Club Championship Show at Stoneleigh and the Federation Show at Stafford have an accumulation of all the breeds, some of whose origins are in this book. Poultry keeping as a hobby is doing far better than it has done for years as people have a yearning to return to the land as an antidote to the pace of modern life.

AUSTRALORP

Like most breeds of poultry, the Australorp began as something else. A large black utility bird was bred by William Cook of Orpington, Kent, around 1886, which he made from Minorca, Black Plymouth Rock, clean-legged Croad Langshan and Black Cochin, all of which were, according to his writings, of no use for breeding according to the standard of the time but put aside only for laying or table
birds. Thus the best utility characteristics were already there and the Black Orpington was promoted as especially suited for residents in towns and manufacturing districts, presumably not only for its production, but also so that it would not show the dirt.

There was a keen demand from Australia for utility fowl in the 1900's and many of William Cook's original stock were exported and kept there for laying and table purposes. By the time they were imported back to Britain in 1921, the Black Orpington in the UK had veered towards the exhibition side and lost most of its utility points. The importers of the Australian Orpingtons were vilified and the most scathing and dismissive comments were printed. Undaunted, the devotees amalgamated the name to Australorp and concentrated on maintaining and developing the birds' laying ability.

By 1936 the breed was near the top of the laying trials and very popular with those wanting a healthy, docile and productive hen. It was recommended that pullets weigh 6lb when at point of lay in order to produce better breeders and layers. The beetle-green sheen on the black feathers was much admired but any birds with a purple sheen were not supposed to be destined for the breeding pen. Leg colour should be uniformly black, although in older birds a lighter colour may be expected, and white soles to the feet. There were also recommendations for breeding with only the tighter feathered specimens. One reason was neatness, more becoming to a true utility bird. In reality it was to maintain the difference between the Australorp and the Black Orpingtons which were rapidly becoming balls of fluff on the show bench.

One very distinctive characteristic of the Australorp, whether in the large fowl or miniature version is the prominence of the eye. You should be able to see the black and bold pupil from behind, or at any angle. The comb is single with even serrations, four to six being the required number, with red earlobes and medium length wattles, rounded at the bottom.

In order to be productive, the body must be deep and broad, giving the impression of a good, solid worker but any tendency to coarseness to be rejected. The skin is particularly fine and white in colour, thus enhancing the table qualities.

Although not prone to broodiness, the Australorp hen will go broody and is useful not only to hatch her own eggs, but for bigger ones such as goose eggs. Her character is usually docile and kind and she will adapt well to most situations. It can be beneficial to set eggs from a more nervous breed under an Australorp as she will steady them down with her placid but still protective and maternal nature.

The Australorp chicks hatch as expected on the 21st day and are large and vigorous. They have white down on the underside and black on their backs. They always have this white down to begin with and then the black feathers grow through it. There should be no white feathers in the older birds. They are strong growers but need good quality feed to maximise their growth potential. The hens come into lay at about seven months. It is no advantage to push them to maturity earlier as you just get small eggs for a longer period. The large eggs which you would expect from an Australorp, which are an attractive mid brown in colour, will then appear from a mature bird, the maximum size being produced by hens rather than pullets. These are the ones from which to breed, thus maintaining the size of the birds.

The modern Australorp has still maintained its production, both by the devotees of the utility characteristics and the exhibitors as, unusually, the utility points are taken into consideration when the birds are judged. The judge should be handling the birds as though for production and not just profusion of feathers so the deep and broad body with good width for egg producing is important. When laying trials were still organised the birds had to have enough breed .points to qualify for club awards before they began their laying stint so all along the utility and breed characteristics have gone hand in hand. This is really an ideal situation as the bird is then adaptable for back yard production, semi-commercial production, the table, and exhibiting. No wonder this good all-rounder has such a strong following.

AUTOSEXING BREEDS

The drive to produce more food after World War One was the originator of this valuable experiment. The awareness of the linked characters of Silver and Gold and Barred and Unbarred plumage already existed in that when a Gold cockerel was mated to a Silver hen, the resulting hens' plumage was gold and the cocks' was silver; the same with the barring factor. What the developers of the Autosexing breeds were trying to do was create a true-breeding breed (a pure breed) which would continue this trait so that the chicks could be sexed by their down colour at day old.

The first successful development was the Cambar, made from the Campine and the Barred Rock.. All the Autosexing breeds take their names from their components, thus the Legbar (Leghorn and Barred Rock), Dorbar (Dorking and Barred Rock), Welbar (Welsummer and Barred Rock), Rhodebar (Rhode Island Red plus barring), Wybar (Wyandotte plus a barred breed), etc. Their further development was cut short by World War Two and the breeds dwindled into very few hands. There was a resurgence in the 1960's and some examples are now at shows. The cockerels of these are often magnificent with the colours allied to the barring but the hens are often dowdy as they have only one dose of the barring factor which has the effect of smudging the markings.

BRAHMA

Harrison Weir devotes no less than 28 pages in "Our Poultry" to the controversy surrounding the arrival, development and naming of the Brahma from 1850 to 1880. It certainly kept the poultry fanciers and printers occupied in trying to unravel the progression of an Asiatic fowl from China, to America, to England which eventually acquired an Indian name. This was at the same time as the Cochin, or Shanghai, had appeared and taken the country by storm with its enormous size. The Brahma was supposed to be bigger still, even when first imported under the name of Chittagong. The original colour was the Light, that is, white body, black striped neck hackle, black in the wings and a black tail. The Dark was developed in the later years of the 19th century and subsequently became more popular on the showbench. In the beginning it was a utility fowl, renowned for its laying capacity but with the development of the profuse but close feathering which we see today, the productive qualities diminished and the Brahma became a Fancier's fowl, even a rich man's fowl in the words of one Edwardian writer as the birds ate a lot and were merely decorative.

The Brahma is a large bodied fowl, which, due to its height, does not appear as full and broad as it actually is. The back is broad and due to the required sweep from hackle to tail, appears shorter than it really is, the hackle being profuse and the saddle rising into the tail which is nearly as high as the head. For such a large bird (cocks 10-12lb, hens 7-9lb) the head is small and neat, but broad over the top of the skull culminating in heavy eyebrows. This does not give the bird a mean look as in the Malay but an aristocratic look in the cock and a coquettish look in the hen. The comb is known as a triple pea which means it looks like three single combs set side by side, very small, with the centre one slightly raised. The earlobes are long and pendulous and should hang as low as the wattles which are small, fine and rounded. In both the Dark and the Light, the hackle should be silver white with a stripe of black in the centre. In the best birds the hackle meets at the front of its neck, whether cock or hen. The wing bows and back of the Dark are silver white, with the saddle feathers having a black stripe. The breast, tail and underparts are all black, ideally free from any white feathers and there is a white wing bar. The breed is heavily feathered on its legs with preferably the soft feathers on its hocks, not the hard feathers (known as vulture hocks) completing the outline. Legs are brilliant yellow in all the colours. A distinctive feature is a slight dip at the back of the skull.

The cock and the hen in the Light have roughly the same distribution of markings but the hen Dark is very different. She has each body feather a clear grey with fine pencilling of darker grey, following the outline of the feather, even and clearly defined. A very delicate and most attractive marking. The old books only mention the Light and the Dark, but there are three more colours which are standardised. These are the White, which is pure white throughout, and the Gold, which was developed from the Partridge Cochin and shares the same clear gold ground colour with the pencilling as in the Dark hen. The cock Gold Brahma is the typical black-red colouring of gold hackles striped with black, solid black breast, gold saddle, black tail and black underparts. The third colour is the Buff Columbian which is identical to the Light, except that the white is replaced with a golden buff.

They are stately, docile, sensible birds who make good broodies, covering a fair number of eggs with their large body size. The egg they lay themselves is small, and there are not many of them, the Lights being probably the better layers. The chicks hatch strongly and feather up quickly and like all feather-legged breeds they are born with down on their legs as well, making identification of them as chicks that much easier. They take about two years to reach their maximum weights so the exhibition birds have to be really mature in order to gain top places and of course they have to be kept out of the sun in order to avoid the yellowing or fading of the feathers which happens even in weak sunlight.

Those who keep Brahmas, even when they do not show them, are totally dedicated to the breed - there is something very special about their character and colours not found in other breeds which appeals to a sense of beauty and stateliness.

COCHIN

What a furore this huge ginger bird caused when it arrived in England from China in 1845. No-one had seen poultry either so large or such an unusual colour and it created a competitive spirit of exhibiting, kudos and 'one-upmanship' that has proliferated ever since. Before the arrival of the Cochin (or Shanghai as it was first called) poultry were merely kept to produce eggs or meat, or to fight for entertainment.

The original birds were given to Queen Victoria which of course helped in their popularity and notoriety. The size of the birds was greatly exaggerated and it was said their crow was like the roar of a lion. Even with the early importations the wealth of feather was in existence as it was believed that the Chinese had developed the breed specifically for filling duvets. It was the Victorians who developed the heavily furnished hock, leg and foot feather that we associate with Cochins today.

The Cochin should not have a sharp angle on it. It is a breed of roundness. Unfortunately the rotundity extends to its metabolism as the birds are prone to fat and heart problems, compounded by their desire to be idle and decorative. Unless kept on short grass they will not venture far and long vegetation tends to break the feathers on the feet. They need little fencing to contain them, however. Although it is lovely to see the feather perfect specimens in the show pens, they are not going to be the fittest as they will have been kept indoors, so when purchasing Cochins a few broken foot feathers will indicate that the bird has been outdoors and is therefore a fitter and possibly better breeder. Even in the early 1900's it was recommended that cocks under three years old were more reliable for breeding.

The Cochin hens, even when young, have a matronly look about them and in fact make excellent broodies, being calm, maternal and able to keep large numbers of chicks warm with the profuse feathering. The number of eggs produced is small (one hundred per year is an excellent average) and the size of the eggs varies with the colours, the Buffs laying the smallest egg, which is surprising as it is generally the largest of the colours. Sometimes it seems incredible that such a huge bird could grow from an egg that a bantam would be proud of.

The chicks hatch reasonably strongly and have the feathering on their legs when born, like all feather-legged breeds. You can see at this stage how well they will be leg-feathered when adult and if the prescribed feathering is all the way down the middle toe. They are so docile that if kept with other breeds they may be pushed off the feed, and they need a lot of very good feed in order to mature, which takes about two years. Once they have got past the teenage vocally complaining stage, they grow steadily.

There is a wide variety of colours available, the most popular and original being the Buff which is a bright ginger all over, down to the skin, free from black feather in the tail. The White is gaining popularity, although of course difficult to keep clean and free from the sappiness (yellow shading) caused by sunshine. The Blue should not be laced, but an even blue all over, the cockerels of course being slightly darker on the hackle and saddle feathers in all the self (single) colours. The Cuckoo is in a few hands and follows the soft alternating colours of grey and dark grey across all the feathers, and the Black has a beautiful green sheen. The Partridge is possibly the most interesting and spectacular of the colours as the cocks and hens are completely different from each other. The cock is the typical storybook colouring of orange-red hackle and saddle with black stripes, black breast and tail with a green sheen but the hen has fine pencilling of dark brown following the shape of the feather on a brown background. This pencilling is most attractive and on good specimens extends from under the chin even to the foot feather. The hackle is gold with a black stripe. The legs of all the colours should be as yellow as possible, although in the dark colours it is not so easy to obtain.

Particular features of the Cochin are the soft and profuse feathering and the enormous and wide cushion that virtually obscures the tail, giving a shape when viewed from the rear of three dinner plates, one set on top of the other two. The older strains of birds tend to have a small dewlap under the chin. There should be no vulture hocks (hard feathers) on the hock of the birds and also no break between the hock feathers and the feathers on the shank. Once the Cochin is mature, the front should drop, well illustrated in the photographs of the birds.

It is now obvious that the Cochin is more decorative than utility; even the meat carrying capacity on such a huge frame is limited due to the short wings and therefore not much breast muscle needed to support them and with weights of 10-13lb in the cock and 9-11lb in the hen, the meat tends to be carried on the legs.

Like the other Victorian passion for topiary and statuary, the Cochin is more a thing of beauty, but has a strong band of devotees and is always admired for its colours, shape and character.

CROAD LANGSHAN

When Major Croad returned from Langshan in China with some chickens in 1872 he can hardly have realised the furore and controversy he, or rather they, would create. The Victorians were still reeling from the sight of the enormous Cochin and tremendous rivalry ensued as to who had the biggest and best. The poultry books of that time contain the most vicious attacks on other breeders, probably those who were winning more prizes. The Croad Langshan, as it was dubbed, was immediately classed as a black Cochin and the devotees of the former spent the next thirty five years proving that it was a separate and distinct breed, so much so that Miss Croad, the Major's daughter, imported more Langshans direct from China on numerous occasions to prevent any accusation of other breeds (ie. Cochins) being crossed with it.

Understanding more about genetics now than in those days, we can see that there were several differences between the two breeds, one of the most obvious being the different coloured legs. All Cochins have yellow legs and those of the Croad Langshan are black with pink soles to their feet. There should also be pink showing between the scales of the Langshan legs. The shape of the two breeds was unfortunately rather similar then, which served to fuel the controversy.

The shape of the Croad Langshan has been refined over the years to maintain its strong utility qualities with a good deep breast carrying a substantial amount of meat, short thighs encouraging tenderness of meat as lanky thighs are usually stringy, and a deep abdomen in the hens for the production of plenty of eggs. One of the most unusual characteristics of this elegant breed is that the tail should be on the same level as the head, both in cocks and hens. This makes a graceful curve to the back, with the small and neat head carried well back. Fineness of bone in such a large bird - males must be at least 9lb - increases the meat capacity and lends an aristocratic air to both cocks and hens. The legs have slight feathering on them, just on the outside and only on the outer toe.

11

The toenails must be white, and black spots on the soles of the pink feet are a serious fault. Some people consider black poultry to be rather dull compared to the more extravagantly coloured breeds, but anyone who has seen the brilliant green sheen on the black feathers of the Croad Langshan cannot fail to be impressed. Unfortunately this wonderful sheen does not reproduce in black and white photography, leaving a visual delight largely untrumpeted. Some birds have a purplish tinge, which is to be avoided in the breeding pen. The eyes should be dark brown or hazel. Any bird producing light eyes is frowned upon from a breeding or exhibiting angle, but would no doubt grace the kitchen just as well.

Brown shelled eggs were unheard of in England before the Croad Langshan was imported and this was the first Asiatic breed to produce them in this country. In fact, the shell colour is brown tinged with plum, no other breed producing this distinctive colour, and the genes for this were introduced in many another breed supposedly to improve the colour by darkening it. Even today, brown eggs are considered to be healthier and more nutritious than any other colour, which is a complete fallacy, being entirely in the eye of the beholder, taste being dependent on the quality of feed.

Breeding the black Croad Langshan is not difficult as the hens are good sitters and very attentive mothers. They can cover at least a dozen eggs as they are so large, and their docility and quietness makes even a beginner successful, whether chicken or human. When the chicks hatch they have a large proportion of white on their undersides - unexpected in a black bird for those who have not seen it before - and like all poultry with accessories (ie. feathered shanks) they are born with feathery down on their legs.

The Croad Langshan breed is fortunate in having a strong and enthusiastic Club which caters for both beginners and exhibitors and insists on maintaining the utility qualities of the breed. The birds did well in laying trials in the 1930's and W. Powell Owen, the doyen of productive birds, considered them to be a good utility fowl. Of course, due to their size, they need a good quality feed but they are keen on foraging and in the summer months will gain many extras from the grass, herbs and insects.

Emphasis has been placed so far on the black variety but there are two more colours, although kept in very much smaller numbers. These are the white and the blue. The white is pure white throughout but maintains the dark legs and the dark eye, and the blue is a delicate shade of slate grey with some black lacing.

There is a miniature version of the Croad Langshan but as miniatures are supposed to be a quarter the size of their large counterparts, the small version is hardly small and makes a very good back yard or small garden breed as its docility means it will take confinement kindly. With a good body weight, there is still scope for culinary usefulness, as well as a good sized egg.

Despite their size, the Croad Langshans are long lived; there is one seven year old miniature hen still taking top prizes at shows and breeding good stock as well. They are bound to keep their popularity with their docility, elegance and usefulness and will proudly grace any garden, farmyard or farm park.

DORKING

There is a resplendent but silent Dorking cockerel resident in the Dorking and District Museum as a fitting testament to this breed's antiquity and popularity. This champion bird was presented in a glass case in the 1970's by the late Mrs Margaret Belyavin, energetic Dorking Club Secretary and staunch supporter of the breed, having taken over the running of the Club from Mr A. J. Major, whose bloodlines of Dorkings are found in all the strains available today.

The antiquity of this breed is documented as far back as 30 AD when the Roman writer, Columella, praised a table bird as being square in shape with sturdy short legs and five toes, the same characteristics desirable in the modern Dorking. Due to the square and meaty body, the Dorking has always been prized for its flesh and eating qualities, including white skin and legs. In the 1860's the speed of growth was an important factor. Whether that speed has now slowed or whether we are blinded by the speed of the broiler is debatable, but flavour and texture have long been valued in the Dorking. Sussex and Surrey have traditionally been the main poultry producing areas for table birds, some being consumed locally and some being sent to London for the discerning gourmets, so the Dorking area has been established as providing first class meat for several centuries.

Unexpectedly, in spite of the low carriage and heavy looks of the Dorking, they are very active and prefer to range widely. With the weights of the adult cocks reaching 12lb it is understandable that they can suffer from bumble foot, an infection of the pad of the foot usually caused by too hasty a descent from high places. The fifth toe does not seem to serve any useful purpose and is placed just above the fourth toe and points upwards. It is a dominant feature and is present in only four other poultry breeds as standard. Any Dorkings not possessing the distinct fifth toe should not be bred from.

The laying capacity of the Dorking is reasonable but tends to be concentrated into the early months of the year. The eggs are a good size and white in colour. As with most heavy breeds of fowl, the earlier they can be hatched in the year, the more likely they are to attain their correct weight. Lack of size is something which needs monitoring constantly if the breed is to maintain its characteristics. A mature Dorking needs to be about two years old to be in its prime and for a stout breed they are fairly long lived: six and seven year old hens are commonplace but sometimes the cocks get less fertile after four years.

The original colour of the Dorking would be the Red, closest to the Jungle Fowl due to its camouflaging properties, particularly for sitting hens. Numbers got perilously low in the 1950's and unfortunately some outcrossing with Welsummers was perpetrated as being beneficial. This could not have been more wrong and damaging: the resemblance to colour was slight, the leg colour was yellow and the shape of the bird was nothing like the Dorking. The Red Dorking is a rich mahogany red in the hackle and saddle of the cock, with black underparts and tail. The hen is a rich red with black tipping on each feather and gold and black striped hackle. The shafts of the feathers are a bright yellow which brightens the whole effect. The comb is single and the legs are of course white, as in all the colours. The most numerous colour is the Silver Grey; a striking combination of pure white hackle and saddle in the cock with black underparts, and the hens are a delicate shade of slate grey on the back, finely pencilled with darker markings, silver hackle striped with black and a salmon breast. It can be difficult to prevent the red colour from creeping round to the shoulders in some strains, but a really good hen will often take precedence over a cock in exhibition prizes.

There are very few breeders of the Dark Dorking now. It is not easy to understand why as they are no less attractive with the straw and black hackle and maroon saddle in the male, black underparts again, and straw and black hackle in the female with a red breast and black tipping on the feathers, the back being very dark with the feather shafts nearly white. The comb in the Dark Dorking is allowed to be either rose or single, creating confusion for beginners. The remaining colours are the White and the Cuckoo. Both of these have rose combs, the White being pure white throughout and the Cuckoo being shades of grey and dark grey bars, neither of which colour is kept in any large numbers but the White being the more numerous. Numbers of Dorkings in exhibitions are not great but members of the Club do try to maintain a variety of colours on show, including Silver Grey Dorking miniatures, recently created.

Dorkings are not difficult to rear but they do like to range at an early age and appreciate being reared in small batches. They are not an aggressive breed and so may be elbowed off the food by more pushy chicks of other breeds. It is vital to allow them to have access to really good quality feed all the time if they are to attain their correct size. They are hardy if ranging but can appear weedy if kept in too confined an area. The pullets should start to lay at about twenty-six weeks, depending on the time of year, and once started they continue through the summer months. Broodiness is a problem if the breeder wants more eggs, but they make good and quiet broodies if allowed to sit.

The Dorking retains its utility qualities of meat production even today but it does take a while to achieve the size required. The main breeders are conservationists who do not wish to see this ancient and noble breed disappear.

FRIZZLE

People pay a lot of money to acquire hair styles similar to what comes naturally to a Frizzle. The origin of this extraordinary looking bird is reputedly Asia, and apparently there were examples found throughout Asia and reported on, probably due to their distinctive appearance, by writers in early Victorian times.

The main feature of the Frizzle is its feather construction and shape. Each feather over the entire body of the fowl curls back and upwards towards the head. Individual feathers have a ragged appearance, but narrow feathers are frowned upon. When Frizzles are bred, they will occasionally throw a straight-feathered bird. This is useful in the breeding pen because eventually the frizzled feather becomes so weak through its construction after generations of breeding Frizzle to Frizzle that the bird appears to have bald patches. By using a straight-feathered bird, bred off Frizzles, about every third generation, the frizzled feather maintains its breadth and strength. This applies both to showing and keeping the breed.

There are not many large Frizzles kept at present; the bantam version seems more popular. They are good layers, however, and rarely sit, but when they do are competent mothers. The egg colour varies from white to tinted. They are well fleshed, being classed as a heavy breed and the weights of the cocks should be 8lb and the hens 6lb when mature. Some of the original imports had rose combs but the single comb has long been standardised with red earlobes and red eyes. There has been a swing towards the continental lyre shaped tail although the British version tends to remain with a tail normal in shape but the feathers are ragged with plenty of side hangers.

Although there are not many different colours of Frizzle seen at shows, there are twelve standardised colours. These range from the self (single) colours of black, blue, buff and white, all of which must be evenly coloured throughout and all ideally with yellow legs, through to some of the Game colour such as pile (red and white) and spangle (brownish with white tips to the feathers). Columbian is also allowed, (see the Light Brahma for the pattern), and red, which is similar to the Rhode Island Red, being mahogany with black tail and black in the wings. The cuckoo has the grey and dark grey striping found in other breeds and the black-red and brown-red are as in the Old English Game.

Despite its strange looks, the Frizzle is a hardy fowl and grows rapidly. When the chicks are hatched they look almost normal but very soon the wing feathers start to grow and they immediately turn outwards, followed by the other body feathers. Feathering seems slower than with other fowl but it does not appear to affect the chicks' ability to keep warm and they will hold their own with other breeds when growing. They are not aggressive but just get on with the business of feeding and exploring in their own way. Due to the shape of the feathers, sexing them at the normal 8-10 weeks by feather shape is not easy, as it is hard to tell the pointed cockerel feathers from the rounded hen feathers when they are growing in all directions. The development of the comb is a useful indicator but it is still possible to be caught out at that age.

The Frizzle is considered by many to be a purely exhibition fowl which is doing the breed a disservice as it lays well and grows well. It is certainly a talking point whenever seen at shows or running in a pen and always attracts attention in whatever colour is seen.

HAMBURG

The original birds which now make up this breed were kept in Lancashire and Yorkshire and the earliest recorded mention is in 1702. Two distinct types evolved: the Lancashire birds, known as Mooneys, had the round black spangling on white background, a coarse head with red earlobes and the cocks tended to be hen feathered (the hackle and tail being similar in shape to a hen). The Yorkshire Pheasant, however, had a neat head with white

earlobes, crescent shaped markings and great style in the cockerels with a full flowing tail. The Mooneys were slightly larger and laid well and it appears that the earliest competitive contests were held with these, with each breeder expounding the virtues of his bird, the judge comparing that with the next and the winner going on to compete with the subsequent bird. Time-consuming but obviously producing great entertainment and fierce passions.

With the increase in communications over the country, the gradual crossing of the two types began, resulting in the Hamburg as is seen now: a very beautiful, stylish bird with a rose comb and straight leader (spike at the back of the comb), white earlobes, a long flowing tail and each feather with a round black spangle on it. This is much the most striking in the Silver Spangled Hamburg. In the earlier shows it was accepted by all exhibitors that a certain amount of thinning of the spangles was necessary so that each one could be seen together with the white. When this activity became classed as faking, birds were then bred to have slightly smaller spangles in order to create the same effect. The cockerels have always posed a problem in that, if they have the correct markings for showing, they tend to breed badly marked pullets. The hackle of the cock should have dagger shaped black tips to it, as with the saddle hackle, then even spangling on his breast right up to the chin and down to the thighs, round spangles on the sickles and tail with a most pleasing effect of the spangles stepping down the top edge of the closed wing. In order to get the correct markings on the pullets, much darker cocks were used but they could not be exhibited. This need to have two different colours of birds to create the standard is known as double mating. You may need double the number of birds to get the required result, as well as doubling up on the breeding pens. It is perfectly possible to breed Hamburgs from the correct looking cock and the correct looking hen; it is only the showbench purists, heading for the top awards, who will take the considerable trouble to double-mate their birds.

The Silver is not the only colour in the spangle; there is the Gold, which has a bay background where it is white in the Silver, but it has a black tail. The Black, which seems to be the only colour to have retained its egg laying capacity, has a beautiful green sheen and the same stylish carriage. The Pencilled varieties were brought in from Holland in the mid 1800's and were known as the Dutch Everyday Layers as they were so prolific, albeit with a smallish egg. Pencilling is an attractive marking with fine black bars going across the body feathers, the background colour being the same width as the bars, and clear colour in the hackle, the two colours being silver and gold.

The chicks of the Silver Spangled and Silver Pencilled are rather a non-descript yellow with a dark back, but the Gold have tigerish brown and yellow stripes. They are very active and feather up quickly. Care should be taken to cull out any which have deformities, as roach back (a hump in the back similar to the fish, the roach) has been a problem in Hamburgs, even from Victorian times. The growers mature quickly as befits a breed classified as Light, but not many attain the standardised weights of 5lb for the cocks and 4lb for the hens. They do best on free range as they are so active and need quite some training to stand quietly in a show pen. They are very good flyers so, for domestic keeping, people tend to clip the primary feathers on one wing, even if only to protect their vegetable garden from being invaded and destroyed.

The large Hamburgs are not as popular as they were, probably due to the fact that their utility qualities have been largely ignored in favour of perfect markings. The miniature, however, thrives and in some quarters is getting so large as to rival the big ones, still laying white eggs.

Unlike so many white and black hens, the legs of the Hamburg are not white or yellow; they are a shade of lead blue which complements the rest of the colouring. In the older books it is mentioned that the skin and flesh are grey which rather damns them for the table. The Hamburg has had many troughs and peaks in its popularity during its long history. It is hoped that the strong following it has at present will continue to promote this most beautiful and graceful breed.

INDIAN GAME

Indian Game are ticklish. Since they are descended from the Asil, which in India means aristocratic, this measure of sensitivity is an indication of their superior breeding. If you lightly scratch an Indian game it will induce it to preen. This is just one of the endearing characteristics of what is at first glance, not an attractive breed.

They have been bred in Cornwall for many hundreds of years and there is a link with the similar Asil in India going back to the Phoenicians, who mined the tin in Cornwall and had much trade with India. Of course the Indian Game has been bred for meat, with its wide breast and good bone structure to carry a lot of flesh, but it differs from its ancestor in that, with the introduction of fresh blood from Malay and Black-Red Game, it has not retained the pugnacity of the Asil. Although the Indian Game looks like a Sumo wrestler, it has not been used for fighting; the Indian has the beetle brows of the Asil, but a much kinder expression.

The whole impression of a good Indian, cocks and hens alike, is of massiveness. The shortness and width of bone in the leg has been steadily developed over this century; the earlier birds were longer on the leg and more rangy, probably due to the Malay influence. Short, stout shanks are desirable in the modern bird but this does not help with fertility as some of the best champions have their legs set so wide apart that they find mating difficult, if not impossible. To have a vigorous cock Indian with the required shanks is a real advantage, and they need to be kept active and encouraged to forage to prevent them from running to fat and becoming unfit. This also applies to the hens and they both suffer from heart and lung problems if kept in a restricted space. They are not as clumsy as they look and, once used to it, will forage with enthusiasm. Controlled feeding helps to keep their weight stable and crushed oats have always been a basic in the Indian diet.

The Standard requires a commanding and courageous bird, combining elegance with substance. The plumage on the females

Dark Brahma cock

Dark Brahma hen

Light Brahma cock

Light Brahma hen

Buff Cochin cock

Buff Cochin hen

Buff Cochin hen

White Cochin hen

Partridge Cochin cockerel

Partridge Cochin hen

Blue Cochin hen

Marsh Daisy cock

Black Croad Langshan cock

Black Croad Langshan hen

White Croad Langshan cock

White Croad Langshan hen

Silver Grey Dorking cock

Silver Grey Dorking hen

Dark Dorking cock

Dark Dorking hen

Red Dorking cock

Red Dorking hen

White Frizzle cock

White Frizzle hen

Indian Game cock

Indian Game hen

Jubilee Game cock

Jubilee Game hen

Black-Red Old English Game cock:
Carlisle type.

Black-Red Old English Game hen:
Carlisle type.

Ginger Old English Game cock:
Carlisle type.

Grey Old English Game hen:
Carlisle type.

Pile Old English Game cock:
Carlisle type.

Blue-Grey Old English Game hen

Crele Old English Game cock: Oxford type.

Black-Red Old English Game: Oxford type.

Silver Spangled Hamburg cock

Silver Spangled Hamburg hen

Black Hamburg hen

Silver Duckwing Modern Game

Black Red Modern Game

Duckwing hen

Ixworth cock

Ixworth hen

Norfolk Grey cock

Norfolk Grey hen

Old English Pheasant Fowl

Old English Pheasant Fowl hen

Black Orpington cock

Black Orpington hen

Buff Orpington cock

White Orpington hen

Blue Orpington cock

Blue Orpington hen

White Crested Black Poland cock

White Crested Black Poland hen

White Poland cock

White Poland hen

Chamois Poland cock

Chamois Poland hen

Light Sussex cock

Light Sussex hen

Speckled Sussex cock

Speckled Sussex hen

Buff Sussex cock

Buff Sussex hen

White Sussex cock

Red Sussex cock

Black Scots Dumpy cock

Black Scots Dumpy hen

Cuckoo Scots Dumpy cock

Cuckoo Scots Dumpy hen

contributes much to this elegance as the feathers are hard and close and most beautifully double laced. This lacing, together with type, carries over half the total points when showing - a poorly laced Indian is a disgrace. The cock bird does not have the lacing but is smart enough with his beetle-green shine on black feathers, and bay colouring throughout, including a triangle of bay showing on the closed wing. The Standard even states how many primary feathers the Indian Game should have - perhaps a tribute to the tenacity and perseverance of the Cornish breeders in aiming for perfection in their creation. The comb is of the pea type (three very small single combs with the centre one raised slightly) and the earlobes and wattles are smooth and fine textured. The legs should be yellow or orange - the deeper colour being more desirable. There are two colours of the Indian game: that previously described is the Dark and the other is the Jubilee. Anywhere that is black on the Dark is white on the Jubilee. The lacing is still required to be perfect and ideally the breast on the Jubilee should be completely white. The bare breastbone is a feature of the breed and shows that the feathering is of the short and hard type.

People with small hands have trouble handling Indian Game; there is just so much of them and with weights of 8lb in the cocks and 6lb in the hens, minimum, and the flesh being so firm, they are literally a good handful. This does not mean that they are awkward in character, in fact quite the reverse, becoming tame and confiding with not much effort on your part. It is always best to start handling any fowl from a young age and the Indian is unique in that at day old its body shape can clearly be seen. This allows for culling or selection at a useful early age as their vigorous appetites certainly contribute to the feed bill. At least they make a very good table bird and breeders usually grow on some culls for just this purpose. The modern broiler owes much to the Indian Game as the traditional meat bird was a cross between an Indian cock, fairly long legged, and a white feathered breed such as the Sussex. Highly prized carcasses were produced with very good fleshing and broad breasts. The Americans, who incidentally re-named the Indian Game the Cornish, both to distinguish it from other Game and as a tribute to the breeders in Cornwall, imported many examples of the bird and during the forties and fifties produced the fast growing meat bird which is on every supermarket shelf.

Housing for Indians need not be elaborate but it is vital to ensure that the pophole is large enough. With their round sides and broad shoulders, the Indian is understandably unhappy at squeezing through small places. Perches should be low in order to avoid bumble foot, an infection which can be caused initially by bruising if jumping down from high places. The low back toe is also subject to injury with high perches.

Although egg production is slight, this meaty breed has a wonderful character and a very strong following all over the country, not only in its native Cornwall, although the mild and sunny climate of the south-west seems to suit them best.

IXWORTH

Developed in the 1930's by Reginald Appleyard of Ixworth, Suffolk, as a good all rounder, with its parentage being Jubilee Indian Game, White Sussex and White Wyandotte. He wanted a breed which was equally good at laying, meat production and broodiness, something which nowadays would not be expected as each breed has its own strong production characteristics. The danger of trying to have everything in one package is that all the traits reduce to mediocrity. Unfortunately, the Ixworth never caught on, the Second World War making people concentrate on more important issues. Its best claim to fame is as a sire for table production as the broad breast, white skin, plumage and legs when crossed with more prolific breeds produced a good carcass. The modern broiler after the War eclipsed any further progress the Ixworth may have made. It is kept in very few hands but those who do keep it are devotees.

MARSH DAISY

Its attractive name belies its appearance, for although made from the Old English Game, Sicilian Buttercup, Malay and Hamburg in the 1930's, the general impression is of a coarse game bird. It is classed as a heavy breed but looks small for the standardised weights of 6lb in the cock and 5lb in the hen. The original colour was wheaten, obviously from the Game influence, but other colours were created by enthusiasts. The only colour seen for many years now has been the wheaten. The earlobes are white and the legs willow green, influenced by the Hamburg and the Buttercup respectively. The wheaten colour is attractive in that the cockerel is gold on the hackle and saddle, tail black with beetle green shine and the rest a golden brown. The hen has chestnut hackle with black tips, a dappled effect back due to the alternation of wheat (straw colour), red wheat and white wheat on the feathers, breast white wheat and tail dull black with red wheat edging. The wings have a bow (upper surface) of red wheat and the flights show a triangular patch of light brown when closed.

The breed was said to be capable of thriving in swampy ground when it was first developed, as well as making a good table bird and having good laying potential. When judging, this laying potential should be taken into consideration in the depth of the abdomen in the hen, providing room for much egg production.

MODERN GAME

The old poultry books are almost without exception derogatory about the development of the Modern Game when there was such a noble bird as the Old English Game gracing the farmyards and gardens of England. It was the outlawing of fighting in 1849 which led to an exhibition bird being developed but Harrison Weir could not understand why all the defects of the Old English Game, such as stilty long legs, small narrow tail, an upright

23

stance and a snaky head, were then exaggerated and considered beautiful in the Modern.

Of course some of those breeding Modern Game for exhibition in the late Victorian times had never been to or participated in a cock-fight and did not appreciate the advantages of the shorter and more powerful Game. Instead they believed that elegance was obtained by the tall, bold springy and hard type of the Modern. Both cocks and hens should look as though they are reaching to their full height and training is given in the showpen with titbits to encourage this "reach". There are more points awarded for style, type and condition than colour and the colours in the Modern Game are fewer than in the Old English. The Black-Red is a popular one as the orange hackle and crimson saddle contrast well with the black breast and thighs in the cock, while the hen is a pretty shade of gold on the neck, salmon on the breast and a delicate shade of ash on the thighs. The body colour is a light partridge brown, finely pencilled, and the tail black.

The introduction of Malay blood to increase the height of the Modern Game has meant that the legs are very long. The fierce Malay expression was bred out and a snaky, long thin head advocated. The Malay influence also gave the Modern the small, narrow tail, held slightly above the line of the back and well whipped (the feathers being closely held together as though bound-whipped-with thread). Apparently the long legs led to a delicacy of constitution and knock-knees (or cow hocks) were a deformity to be avoided, together with a crooked breastbone, obvious only if the bird is handled. They get tame and steady quite quickly but do not take kindly to being confined for any length of time. Training for the showpen would then be done at intervals of a few days with the birds running out in between. The shoulders should be broad and well forward, the body short, the back flat and tapering to the tail. The feathers should be very short and hard, the cock's hackle feathers being particularly favoured by dry fly fisherman. The colour of the legs varies with the plumage colour, but the shanks should be rounded with the back toe standing out well behind.

The Modern Game was such a novelty in the 1880's that cocks changed hands for £100, a great deal of money in those days. When breeding them it was said that they did best under a broody hen, presumably because of the exercise for those long legs, and a cockerel under twelve months of age was not recommended for best fertility. The most striking colour in the male is possibly the

Pile. There are few birds with red and white colouring in poultry and the cock has a hackle of bright orange-yellow, the back and saddle a rich maroon, wing bow maroon and the secondaries dark chestnut, showing when the wing is closed, all else being pure white. The female is much duller with a gold wash over the hackle, salmon red breast and the rest white. The Brown-Red is almost a misnomer as the only colours allowed in it are lemon and black in both cocks and hens. The Birchen is an attractive pattern as the top plumage in the cock is silver, the rest black, with delicate lacing on the breast feathers. The hen has silver hackle and the same delicate breast lacing. Both have gypsy (dark) faces with black eyes. The other colours are the Duckwings, both golden and silver and at one time there were some self coloured (single colour) varieties of white, black and blue.

There has always been a devoted following of the Modern, provoking endless discussions over type and colour and although they seem to be an acquired taste, they have survived strongly over the years.

NORFOLK GREY

Just one of the many new breeds created between the two World Wars that is still fairly popular, although in few hands, this attractively marked heavy breed was made by a Mr Myhill of Norwich by apparently crossing Birchen Game and Silver Duckwing Leghorns. The shape is very different from both its parents, being rather blocky, the weights being 7lb on the cocks and 5lb on the hens. The purpose of producing this breed followed a trend to have something different to show and with the table attributes and brown egg of the Norfolk Grey, it deservedly continued as a breed, most of the other creations of that time falling by the wayside. It very nearly missed, however, as its originator called it the Black Maria; even when pronounced as Mareea as he intended, the funereal connotations together with the colour of the bird were a recipe for disaster, so it was quickly re - christened the Norfolk Grey.

The cock has silver hackle striped with black on its neck, back, saddle and wing coverts, the rest a rich black. The hen has hackle similar to the cock but the rest of the plumage a rich black, with the throat very delicately laced with silver for about two inches.

This is the birchen influence, of course, and the Leghorn influence can be seen in the medium-sized, single, upright comb with large serrations. The legs are black, as are the eyes, and the earlobes are red.

The Norfolk Grey breeds well and is a usefully productive bird, as well as being active and smart, and so should retain reasonable numbers among poultry keepers.

OLD ENGLISH GAME

When the Romans first came to these shores they found certain domestication of poultry, but the main use was for entertainment or sport, not so much for meat. The practice of cockfighting is a very ancient one, documented all over the world for the past 2,000 years. For something so ingrained in daily life, it must have been a real blow when cockfighting was outlawed in 1849. Everyone used to be involved, from royalty down to schoolboys who used to pay the schoolmaster a fee on Shrove Tuesday, in order that they could bring their cocks to school and fight them for the day: it certainly enhanced the meagre salary. The fines imposed on the banning of cockfighting were sufficient to deter most, but some never stopped and surreptitiously continued the so called sport. At about the same time, exhibiting was in its infancy, so what better than to direct all the cockfighting energy into showing - competition of a less terminal nature. Many of the characteristics and traditions of the cockfighters were carried into exhibiting, such as the dubbing of the comb. This was vital when fighting as the small single comb was used by the cocks to hold onto their adversary, while inflicting severe damage with the wings and spurs. The practice of cutting off the comb close to the head when the bird was about six months old removed this advantage and prevented much bloodshed. The wattles were also removed for the same reason. An Old English Game cock undubbed looks very peculiar.

Being classed as a non-sitter does not necessarily mean they are flighty: alert and active, yes, but, with a small amount of training, they are perfectly capable of standing in a show pen without fuss. There is usually a strong class at the National Championship Show (December) with the Scots competing against the English, and of course there is a miniature version of the breed which attracts many followers. The shape of the miniature is more blocky than the large due to the influence of other breeds in its make-up, but it is a good layer and quiet enough for children to manage.

With birds kept outdoors, as most Scots Greys will be, there is a tendency for the sun to make the feathers on the cockerel go brassy on his neck and saddle. Running birds in shade or woodland gets over this problem if exhibiting is the goal, but then there may be another problem of enticing them back into the safety of the henhouse at night with all those lovely roosting places in the trees to choose from. Any brassiness on a young bird which has not long been in the sun is to be avoided.

The illustration shows that the barring of the feathers is a very precise affair and results in a beautifully smart and crisp looking bird. The colour is steel grey with a metallic lustre on a lighter background and the bird should "read" throughout, i.e. the shade should be the same from the head through to the tail. The barring is straight across the feather on the body, thighs and wings, and of equal width, but on the neck hackle, saddle and tail slightly angled or V-shaped, each feather ending in a black tip. The females are not quite so precisely marked and their markings are larger, lending themselves more to the tartan effect. The beak should be white or white streaked with black and the legs white, or, in the more aristocratic lines, white with black mottles.

You may think that all this long-legged leaping over heather would make the bird tough and stringy, but although the breast meat is not over generous on the Scots Grey, it is valued for being particularly full of flavour with good texture and pure whiteness of skin. Age of bird makes a difference, of course, but a young bird up to about eight months of age makes a good meal as it should attain 6lb in weight by then if a cockerel.

It sounds as though there ought to be a link between the Scots Grey chicken and the Royal Scots Grey regiment. Some of the officers have made a point of keeping Scots Greys when not serving abroad, and appreciate their qualities.

The Scots Grey is a breed of great antiquity and usefulness. It has many features not seen in other breeds, and indeed, when judging them the judge has to bear in mind the clause in the Standard which reads: any characteristic of any other breed not applicable to the Scots Grey to be a serious defect. The beauty and utility of this fine breed has long and unfairly been neglected in favour of the vagaries of fashion. It deserves to be more widely kept and recognised.

SUSSEX

It may be that people in Southern England were keener on good quality meat than in other parts of the country, as that is where the Sussex was developed in the 1850's. There were several types of poultry at that time variously known as Kent, Sussex, Dorking and Surrey fowls. They began in the black-red colouration as that was the most successful, the females being well camouflaged when sitting. White sports were encouraged to produce a clean finish with no dark stubs on the table bird, and gradually the Sussex came to be generally recognised as a distinct breed with fine table qualities.

The original colours of Sussex mentioned in books of the mid 1800's are the Brown, Red and Speckled. The Brown and the Red are colours with only a few breeders now, and the Speckled is mahogany with small black then white spots on the end of each feather - a most attractive combination. It can be seen how the paler colours arose as the Speckled will moult whiter every year. The Light is probably the best known colour today with its collar of black hackle and black tail and wings. This was the colour used in the first sex-linkage crosses with the Rhode Island Red in the 1920's. Genetically, the Light Sussex is not a white bird but a silver one, so when a male Rhode Island Red was used (genetically gold), the progeny at day old were coloured gold/brown for female and yellow/white for male, the colours crossing over from the mated colours. If the mated colours are reversed, the genetics do not have the same convenient effect, thus it is only the gold

40

male on the silver female which produces the sex-linked chicks. Other sex-linked factors were later discovered such as the barring pattern, but the ground work was done with the Sussex.

Having stated that the Light Sussex is not genetically white, there is also a White Sussex in its own right. This is pure white with the white legs common to all the colours, but does not have such a large following as the Light. The other colour of Sussex which is popular is the Buff. This has the same black feather pattern as the Light Sussex (known in all breeds as the columbian pattern) but with the body colour a rich shade of ginger (buff columbian). Like all buff coloured poultry, ducks, geese and turkeys, the colour fades in the sun until the next moult, so they are at their best when just moulted or kept in shady areas.

In Victorian times the Sussex was preferred to the slower growing and more boney Dorking for meat production and of course they still laid a few eggs. Much was subsequently done to improve the egg production, but this was at the expense of size and weight. The best utility strains nowadays combine the two, making a truly dual purpose bird in the Light Sussex. The Speckled is a poor layer but has good size and a very strong propensity to be broody. If allowed to hatch eggs they make wonderful mothers and are large enough to cover five goose eggs comfortably. The Light Sussex will go broody occasionally but not as often as the other colours. The eggs laid by the Lights, and we expect about 250 a year, are known as tinted, which means they range in colour from creamy white to pale brown. As with all the large fowl heavy breeds, second year hens are best to breed from. With the exception of the Speckled Sussex, which can be rather weedy, the others feather up quickly, and as long as they are allowed to range on good grass they are usually very hardy and mature and grow fast. They are a docile breed and so will mix with others when being reared quite amicably.

One of the early attempts to improve meat quantity was when the Light Sussex hens were crossed with an Indian Game cockerel: these birds are almost square. This produced the shape of the modern broiler but without its rather indecent speed of growth. The slow growing Sussex/Indian Game cross, run outside on free range has an unsurpassed flavour, texture and quality.

The most popular exhibition bird is the Light Sussex and even more so in the miniature version, which incidentally is an excellent layer. The best large exhibition Lights look magnificent with more abundant black in the hackle but are useless as production birds, a good layer losing that "bloom" which can denote a show champion, all other breed points being correct. In the judging of Sussex one quarter of the points is given for "type and flatness of back" which is unique in the British Poultry Standards and bears testimony to its origins as a table bird.

The Sussex in all its colours is in little danger of being swept under the economic carpet by the commercial hybrids when people consistently ask for and want to keep a dual purpose, attractive bird: in fact, a proper looking chicken.

INDEX